FAST Lane
DRAG RACING

PRO STOCK MOTORCYCLE
DRAGSTERS

By Tyrone Georgiou

Gareth Stevens
Publishing

Please visit our Web site, www.garethstevens.com. For a free color catalog of all our high-quality books, call toll free 1-800-542-2595 or fax 1-877-542-2596.

Library of Congress Cataloging-in-Publication Data

Georgiou, Tyrone.
 Pro stock motorcycle dragsters / Tyrone Georgiou.
   p. cm. — (Fast lane: Drag racing)
 Includes index.
 ISBN 978-1-4339-4704-9 (pbk.)
 ISBN 978-1-4339-4705-6 (6 pack)
 ISBN 978-1-4339-4703-2 (library binding)
1. Motorcycle racing—Juvenile literature. 2. Drag racing—Juvenile
literature. I. Title.
 GV1060.G46 2011
 796.72—dc22

                                   2010035245

First Edition

Published in 2011 by
Gareth Stevens Publishing
111 East 14th Street, Suite 349
New York, NY 10003

Designer: Daniel Hosek
Editor: Greg Roza

Photo credits: Cover, pp. 1, 13 Rusty Jarrett/Getty Images; pp. 5, 7, 17, 19 Brian Bahr/Getty Images; pp. 9, 11, 15 (main image) Shutterstock.com; p. 15 (inset) Jonathan Ferrey/Getty Images.

Printed in the United States of America

CPSIA compliance information: Batch #CW11GS: For further information contact Gareth Stevens, New York, New York at 1-800-542-2595.

CONTENTS

Words in the glossary appear in **bold** type the first time they are used in the text.

LET'S DRAG RACE MOTORCYCLES!

People race motorcycles in many different ways—on roads, on dirt, and even on ice and snow. From the earliest days of motorcycle racing, people have tried to see how fast they could go in a straight line over a set distance. Drag racing motorcycles on ¼-mile (400-m) tracks started in the 1950s and 1960s. The National Hot Rod Association (NHRA) Pro Stock Motorcycle Championship Series began in 1987. Over time, Pro Stock motorcycles have become very fast machines.

Fast Fact In 1907, airplane pioneer Glenn Curtiss became known as the "fastest man on Earth." He set the land speed record of 136.4 miles (219.5 km) per hour on a motorcycle of his own design.

Three-time NHRA Pro Stock Motorcycle Champion Andrew Hines lines up for a race in July 2010.

5

WHAT'S A PRO STOCK MOTORCYCLE?

Pro Stock motorcycles look like street motorcycles, or bikes as they're often called. However, they're built for racing. Their engines create 300 **horsepower** (HP) or more. This power speeds them down the track in under 7 seconds!

A drag racing motorcycle must be aerodynamic. This means air flows smoothly over it and doesn't slow it down. The driver and front of the bike need to cut cleanly through the air. To help make this happen, the driver leans forward over the bike.

Pro Stock motorcycles can reach a top speed of 197 miles (317 km) per hour.

Fast Fact

Which flies faster when thrown—a square brick or a smooth, flat stone? The stone, of course. Just like a flat stone, a Pro Stock motorcycle must be smooth to allow air to move easily over its surfaces.

LIGHTWEIGHT BIKES

Pro Stock motorcycles are based on street bikes, such as Harley-Davidsons, Suzukis, and Kawasakis. They have lightweight steel frames that can be changed to make the **wheelbase** longer or shorter. This allows the bike to change to suit different track conditions.

The driver can shift through seven gears with a button on the handlebar. A computer helps control the engine. It also stores **data** that can be sent to the team's computer after each race.

Pro Stock motorcycle bodies are made to look like street motorcycles. However, they're made from **carbon fiber**, which is stronger and lighter than steel.

Pro Stock motorcycle bodies have smooth surfaces and round edges. This helps the bike go faster.

STICKY TIRES

Pro Stock motorcycle tires are smooth and sticky to help speed the bike down the track. The front tire is only used to steer the motorcycle. The **shock absorbers** on the front help the driver keep the motorcycle under control during the race.

The rear tire is bigger than the front tire because the engine sends all the power to it. It's 10 inches (25.4 cm) wide! There are no rear shock absorbers. This helps keep the rear tire in contact with the track surface.

The back tire spins so quickly at the beginning of a race it makes smoke!

Fast Fact
Matt and Andrew Hines are two motorcycle drag racing brothers who each hold three NHRA national championships.

MOTORCYCLES ON THE TRACK

To get the best **traction**, drivers do a "burnout" to heat up their rear tires and the track. Water is sprayed on the track. The drivers **rev** their engines and drive through it. This makes a lot of smoke and noise!

Even with their wide rear tires, Pro Stock motorcycles can be very hard to handle. It takes great skill to control them during burnouts and when going down the track at top speed.

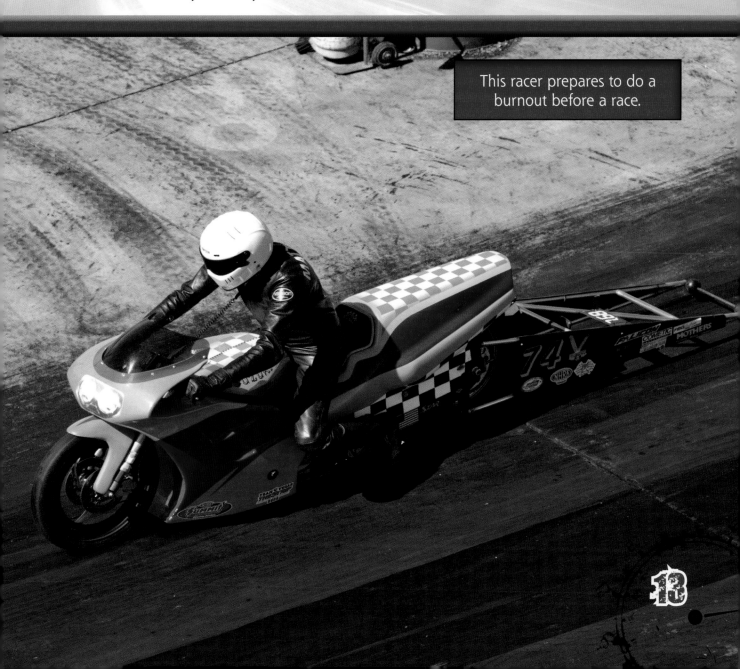

Fast Fact

Dave Schultz is the most successful driver in the history of Pro Stock motorcycle racing with 45 career wins and 6 championships.

This racer prepares to do a burnout before a race.

13

RACE TIME!

When it's time to race, the drivers must get into place on the starting line so they start from exactly the same position. This is called staging. Lights on the starting tree guide the process. Drivers are given the green light to start. If a driver leaves the starting line too soon, they "red light" and lose the race before they even get started. A driver needs a good **reaction time** to win races.

Fast Fact

Angelle Sampey was the first woman champion in Pro Stock motorcycle racing. She retired in 2010 with 41 career wins and 3 national championships.

Angelle Sampey

The starting tree holds the starting lights for a race, which stick out like branches on a tree. It's also called the Christmas tree.

15

Winning a race takes more than hitting the gas. Drivers need to know the right time to shift gears. They must steer their Pro Stock bike down the track without losing control or losing the race. Once they cross the finish line, drivers need to immediately slow their bike down from 190 miles (306 km) per hour to 0. Pro Stock motorcycles use **parachutes** to catch air in order to slow down. This keeps the bike from flying off the end of the track!

Michael Phillips celebrates after setting the world speed record of 197.65 mph (318.09 kmh) on July 18, 2010.

Fast Fact In the drag racing world, using parachutes to stop is called "popping the chutes."

BETWEEN THE RACES

The starting, stopping, and high speeds during a race are hard on a Pro Stock motorcycle. Each bike must be rebuilt after every race! Each **mechanic** on the team has a job to do. The engine is taken apart and gets new parts. The parachutes are repacked. The bike is refueled. Any mistake during this process could lead to problems and even danger in the next race. Computers are used to make sure the motorcycle is ready to go.

Racers are judged on their speed, but also their elapsed time (ET). That is the amount of time it takes to get from the starting line to the finish line.

wheelie bar

Fast Fact

The back tire of a Pro Stock bike creates anough traction at the start of a race to pop the front end up into the air. A "wheelie bar" keeps this from happening.

PRO STOCK MOTORCYCLE SAFETY

Safety issues are much different when racing motorcycles than when racing cars. Car drivers are surrounded by metal and padding. A motorcycle driver can be thrown off the bike and hit the road or another object. Drivers wear full leather racing suits with special plastic **armor**. Should the driver fall off the bike at a high speed, the suit protects the driver's body from cuts and scrapes. A special helmet protects the driver's head in case of a crash.

PRO STOCK MOTORCYCLE NUMBERS

Fastest ET	6.815 seconds, Andrew Hines, 9/4/10
Fastest Speed	197.65 mph (318.09 kph), Michael Phillips, 7/8/10
Most Wins	45, Dave Schultz
First Pro Stock Motorcycle Champion	1987 (NHRA), Dave Schultz
Most Championships (NHRA)	6, Dave Schultz

GLOSSARY

armor: a hard layer of clothing that guards the wearer from harm

carbon fiber: a hard type of cloth that can be heated and formed into shapes. It is stronger and lighter than steel.

data: facts and figures

horsepower (HP): the measure of the power produced by an engine

mechanic: a person who works on cars or motorcycles

parachute: a specially shaped piece of cloth that collects air to slow something down

reaction time: how long it takes to decide to do something

rev: to increase the speed of the engine

shock absorber: a part on a car or motorcycle that makes the ride less bumpy

traction: the stickiness between two surfaces, such as a tire and the track

wheelbase: the distance between the centers of the two wheels

FOR MORE INFORMATION

Books

Graham, Ian. *Super Bikes*. New York, NY: Franklin Watts, 2001.

Lee, Keith. *Drag Bike Racing in Britain: From the mid 60s to the mid 80s*. Dorchester, England: Veloce Publishing, 2010.

Web Sites

Dragbike Network
www.dragbike.com
Read the latest news about Pro Stock motorcycle racing's biggest stars.

The National Hot Rod Association (NHRA)
www.nhra.com
The Web site for the largest drag racing governing body has information on the hottest Pro Stock drivers.

INDEX